BIOTICS

WART ROSS

Text by Stewart Ross in cooperation with Christine Clover.
© copyright in this edition Tulip Books 2019

The right of the Author to be identified as the Author of this work
has been asserted by the Author in accordance with the Copyright,
Designs and Patents Act 1988.

ISBN 978-1-78388-150-5

Index

Germs!

Germs are tiny, tiny creatures that sneak into our bodies. When they get inside, they make us ill.

Germs are so small we can see them only with a **microscope.** »

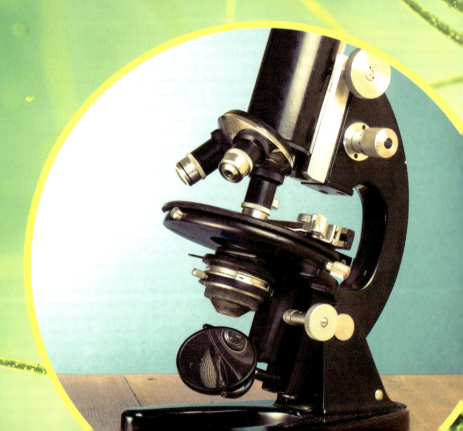

WOW!

One million germs laid out in a row would stretch to just one metre!

Bacteria

One family of germs is known as bacteria. They live almost everywhere, in the soil, in water and in animals.

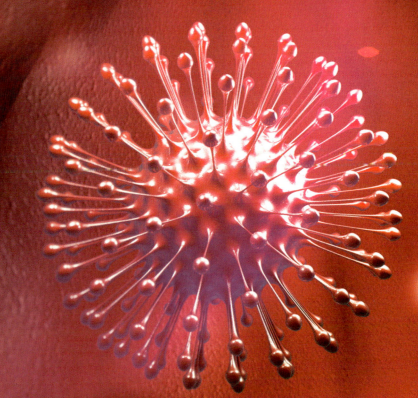

» Most bacteria are harmless. But about 100 types of bacteria can make us very unwell.

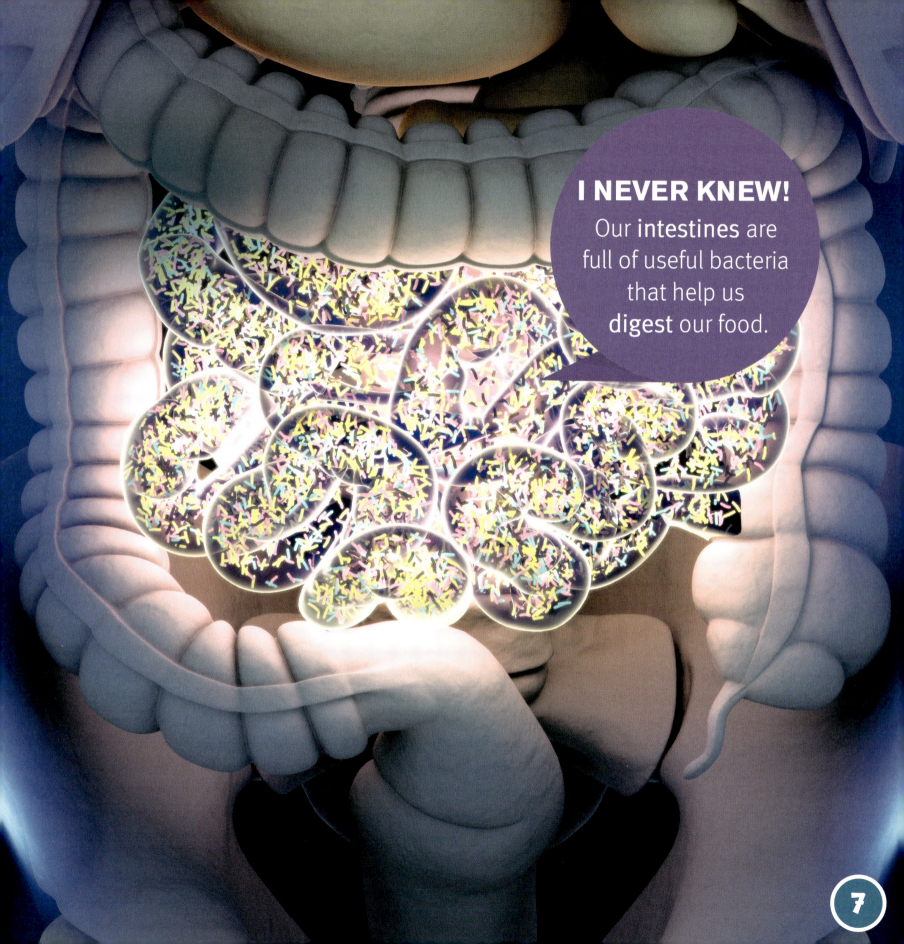

I NEVER KNEW!
Our **intestines** are full of useful bacteria that help us **digest** our food.

Through the microscope

In 1676, a Dutch scientist built a microscope and examined pond water.

I NEVER KNEW!

The word bacterium was invented in 1828; bacteria is the plural, meaning lots of these mini creatures.

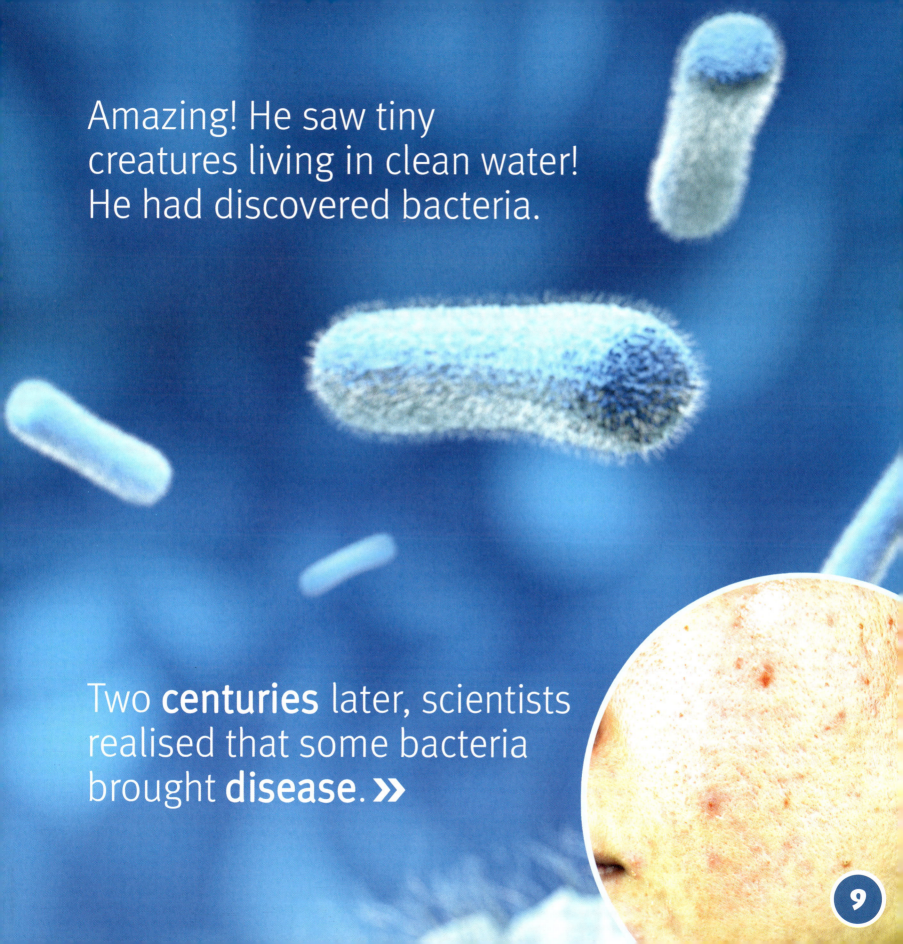

Amazing! He saw tiny creatures living in clean water! He had discovered bacteria.

Two **centuries** later, scientists realised that some bacteria brought **disease**. »

Killer bacteria

By 1910, doctors knew bacteria caused horrible diseases such as: **meningitis**, **tuberculosis**, **pneumonia**, **tetanus**, and **leprosy**.

« Washing and keeping clean stopped these diseases spreading. But doctors were unable to cure them.

I NEVER KNEW!
In the old days, people believed tuberculosis was spread by vampires!

11

Mouldy research

Ancient peoples knew some types of **mould** helped cure **infection**.

A 19th-century doctor found no bacteria on mouldy blue cheese!

Scientists were learning that mould could kill bacteria, but they didn't know why.

I NEVER KNEW!
Bacteria have been living on the Earth for about 3 million years!

Mould juice

In 1928, Dr Fleming left open dishes of bacteria in his **laboratory**. When he returned, one dish had mould on it – and the bacteria were dead.

I NEVER KNEW!

Dr Fleming nicknamed penicillin 'mould juice'!

Fleming found the mould contained penicillin – the world's first antibiotic.

15

Making penicillin

Fleming wrote about his discovery of penicillin, but no one took much notice.

I NEVER KNEW!

'Antibiotic' means 'against life'!

PENICILLIN

He was unable to make it into a drug for doctors to use. Other scientists finally managed this in 1940.

More antibiotics

Now scientists knew how antibiotics worked, they were able to make powerful new ones.

I NEVER KNEW!

When Fleming first saw that penicillin killed bacteria, he said, 'That's funny!'

18

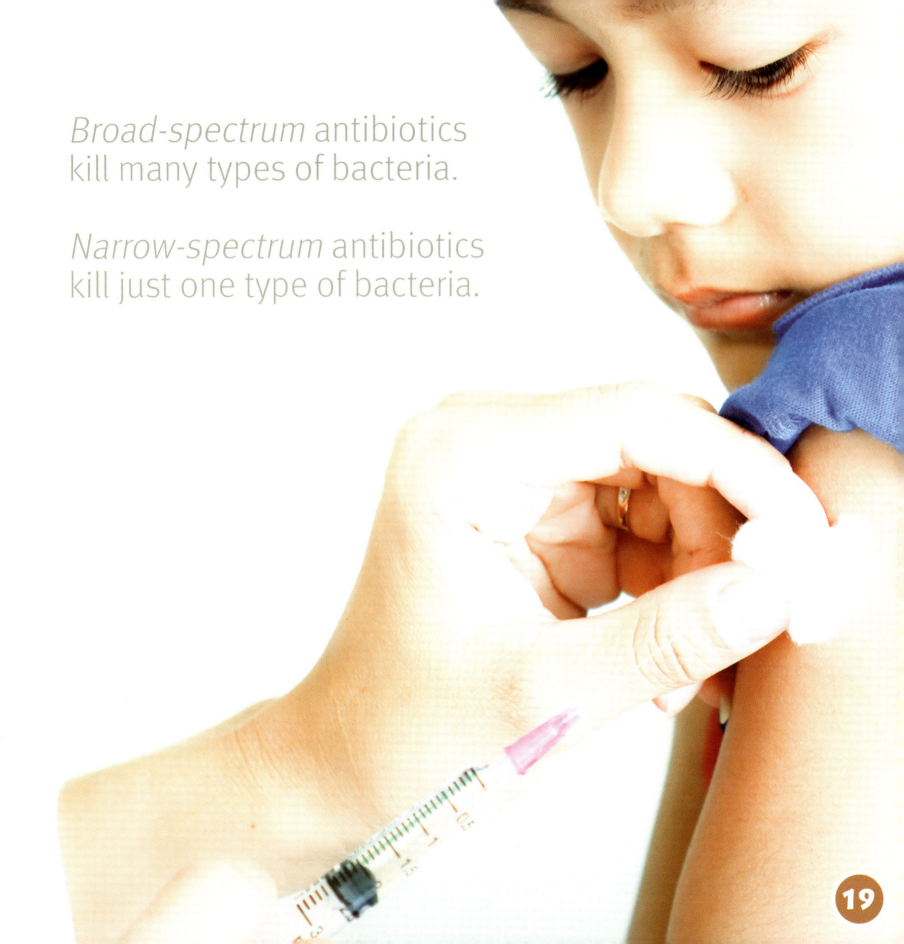

Broad-spectrum antibiotics kill many types of bacteria.

Narrow-spectrum antibiotics kill just one type of bacteria.

19

Antibiotics at work

Antibiotics changed medicine for ever.
Killer diseases, like tuberculosis,
meningitis and pneumonia,
could be cured.

Antibiotics allowed cuts and
sore throats to heal more easily.
Surgery was safer, too, because
antibiotics prevented infections.

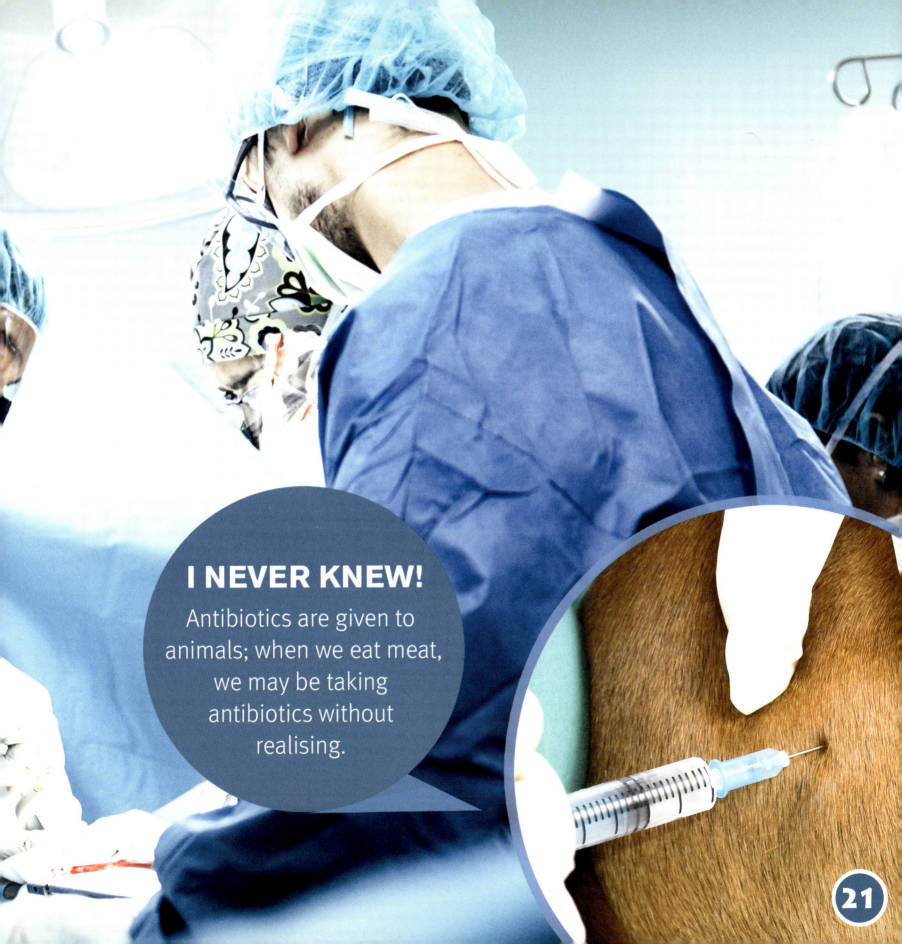

I NEVER KNEW!

Antibiotics are given to animals; when we eat meat, we may be taking antibiotics without realising.

Resistance

Bacteria are great survivors.
They can change so antibiotics
no longer kill them.

We say they become
resistant to antibiotics.

This is a problem for doctors and scientists: new antibiotics are needed all the time.

I NEVER KNEW!
If a course of antibiotics is not finished, the bacteria's resistance grows.

23

Glossary

Century
100 years.

Digest
To take the food we have eaten into our bodies.

Disease
An illness.

Infection
When bacteria get into the body and start causing harm.

Intestines
The long tube inside the body that digests food.

Laboratory
A specially equipped room where research takes place.

Leprosy
A serious disease of the skin and nerves, caused by bacteria

Meningitis
A serious illness of the brain, caused by bacteria.

Microscope
A magnifying machine for examining things that the eye cannot see.

Mould
A fungus that grows on something rotten.

Pneumonia
A serious disease of the lungs, caused by bacteria.

Surgery
Cutting open the body to cure an illness or injury.

Tetanus
A serious disease of the muscles, caused by bacteria.

Tuberculosis
A serious disease of the lungs, caused by bacteria.